WEIGHT TRAINING

for

CYCLING

The Ultimate Guide

WEIGHT TRAINING

for

CYCLING

The Ultimate Guide

CHRIS BURNHAM

**PRICE WORLD
PUBLISHING**

Prior to beginning any exercise program, you must consult with your physician. You must also consult your physician before increasing the intensity of your training. The information in this book is intended for healthy individuals. Any application of the recommended material is at the sole risk of the reader, and at the reader's discretion. Responsibility for any injuries or other adverse effects resulting from the application of any of the information provided within this book is expressly disclaimed.

Published by Price World Publishing
3971 Hoover Rd. Suite 77
Columbus, OH 43123-2839
www.PriceWorldPublishing.com

Cover Design by Russell Marleau
Layout Design by Merwin Loquias
Editing by Wendy Thornton
Photographs by Cindy Burnham
Modeling by Chris Burnham
Printing by Versa Press, Inc.

ISBN: 978-1-932549-874
eBook ISBN: 978-1-619844-209

LCCN: 2015951006

Printed in the United States of America
10 9 8 7 6 5 4 3 2 1

For information about discounts for bulk purchases, please contact info@ priceworldpublishing.com.

Table of Contents

Foreword by Ben Greenfield

If you look at the training methods of the best athletes and teams on the face of the planet, you'll notice that they spend what seems to be an inordinate amount of time doing something other than their actual sport.

Take an NFL football player, for example.

During a four month internship at Duke University, I worked with the Kansas City Chiefs on training and rehab for some of their standout offensive linemen. On any given day, these players wouldW spend an hour in the weight room, 30-45 minutes performing mobility drills, 20-30 minutes engaged in recovery protocols, and then 2-3 additional hours of actual practice.

Or look at an elite swimmer. In one interview, swimmer Dara Torres described her day as follows:

"...when I'm home in Florida I get up at about 6:45 and walk my dog. Then I get my 5-year-old daughter up and feed her, then head off to practice. I start swimming at 8. I'll swim anywhere from an hour to an hour and 45 minutes. Then I'll do some weights and sometimes resistance work for a while followed by lunch. After that I do about two hours of Ki-Hara stretching...."

Let's be realistic, most of us are not Olympic athletes prepared to devote our lives to training, eating and recovering. We have to squeeze in work, meal preparation, chauffeuring kids, mowing the lawn and doing everything else that life throws at the average endurance athlete. By the time we include cycling, is there really time left over for all this other stuff?

And let's face it: to a true endurance junkie it's simply not glamorous or enticing to balance on one leg while lifting a heavy object overhead, learning how to properly perform a lateral lunge, or figuring out what the heck a plyometric is.

The unfortunate reality is that the line of thinking that keeps you only cycling is the same line of thinking as someone who:

- drives a car (or bicycle) into the ground and never maintains their vehicle with anything even so slight as an oil change, then throws up their hands in despair when the engine starts smoking...

- never visits the doctor, never pays attention to their health, or does any preventive tests, then gets frustrated and confused when they get sick or have to shell out money for an emergency visit...

-   expects their home appliances such as the washer, dryer, stovetop, oven or dishwasher to simply always work with zero maintenance, and then is forced to spend an entire paycheck on an expensive repair...

You get the idea.

When it comes to training for endurance, it's very easy instead to get caught up in the endless miles on the bike, while neglecting the stuff that actually keeps our bodies able to do what we love. So while you don't need to spend all your precious hours hoisting a barbell or jumping onto a box, you simply can't be a complete slack-off when it comes to preparing your body adequately for hammering the pedals.

Strength training is just like changing the oil on your car. In a sense, it is a necessary maintenance to stay healthy. Want an example of how lack of strength can hold you back?

Look at a Kenyan marathoner. There's a reason you simply don't see these guys or girls dominating a sport like the Ironman Triathlon. Despite their aerobic superiority, they simply don't have the leg muscle strength to generate the power necessary to move a bicycle 140.6 miles. For this same reason, professional Ironman triathletes tend to be slightly more muscular than their relatively slight, shorter-distance counterparts.

Some would argue that muscle is just extra bulk. It's certainly true that it is not necessary for an endurance athlete to build rippling muscles capable of producing enormous amounts of force. Since muscle takes significant amounts of energy to cool and carry, there is without doubt a point of diminishing returns as an aerobic athlete builds muscle.

I personally experienced the disadvantage of muscle bulk when I began to transition to participating in triathlons from the sport of bodybuilding. Some of my most painful memories of endurance competition came from the soreness, dehydration, overheating and overall discomfort associated with carrying over 25 pounds of "extra" show muscle. But as you will learn in this book, muscle mass is not necessarily synonymous with strength.

What is presented herein is a solid program to build that resilience, that power, that strength that can allow you to maximize your potential as a cyclist. Of course, don't ever neglect your health in the pursuit of your sport. Just strive to be better!

Ben Greenfield, MS, CSCS
Author of *Weight Training for Triathlon: The Ultimate Guide*
BenGreenfieldFitness.com

Chris Burnham

Introduction

That image of the svelte tiny cyclist, dancing on the pedals, climbing the Alpine pass in the Tour de France is so iconic to the sport of cycling, but how much does that represent the goals of most cyclists? We all want to climb like Grand Tour winner, Alberto Contador Velasco, but are we willing to sacrifice health and live that deleterious lifestyle? Limiting calories, spending 30+ hours a week on your bike, and resting all the other hours is what it takes to be a top level professional cyclist. But is that practical or ideal for the rest of us who ride our bikes for fun rather than to make a living?

While pro cyclists have a massive aerobic engine and can put out more power than a John Deere tractor, a key feature of being a professional cyclist is the small frame of the rider since power to weight ratio is one of the biggest determinants of success in the Pro peloton, the main group of riders in a professional biking race. This is the equivalent of taking a Formula 1 engine and dropping it into a Toyota Tercel. Nothing against the Toyota, but the chassis would be too weak to handle the massive torque and horsepower that a Formula 1 engine could produce. It would twist and crumble under the torque. Pro cyclists can get away with the reduced muscle mass partly due to the sport self-selecting genetic freaks, but also because being a pro cyclist is a finite occupation. There is a reason that most pro cycling teams have chiropractors on staff.

If your goal is to be as healthy as possible for as long as possible, then modeling your life after a pro cyclist isn't your best bet. If you are making a living off of racing your bike, then by all means, live the clandestine lifestyle and avoid picking up anything heavier than 15 pounds. Sacrificing muscle mass for your sport is what you need to do if that determines your bottom line, but I would argue that for the rest of us, we can still be very good competitive cyclists, make better overall health choices, and add in some extra muscle mass. We should have a higher priority on the "long game" in our health and quality of life. Strength training, mobility work, and learning how to move better can be very beneficial later in life.

I also feel that there are some professional cyclists who would find more watts per kilograms if they spent a part of their year focusing on strength. Not all who have been blessed with the big aerobic engines have also been blessed with the genetics that give them an inherently strong chassis. Spending some time on the infrastructure of the body may result in better power transfer to the pedals, especially at the end of long races, or at the end of a long season.

In my cycling career this is exactly what I experienced. After suffering a separated shoulder from a mountain bike crash, I headed to the gym to work on some rehab and strengthening my shoulder. I was still convinced that the ideal cyclist was that skinny-armed cyclist climbing the Alps, so I tried to limit any muscle gains and just focus on form and improving shoulder function. Since I had already braved the gym, which as a skinny cyclist isn't always the easiest thing to do, I decided to throw in a few lower body movements to see if it would help my power on the bike. After three months I was pretty disappointed to see that I had gained about four pounds. I thought for sure that my race season would suffer. But what resulted from this small experiment was the best season I ever had up to that point. I felt amazing and finished the season with a lot of podiums, and without the small back aches and upper body pains that would come from a full season of mountain biking.

For many years afterward, I continued to refine this weight program for both myself, but also for my teammates. I read as many journals as I could. I took numerous physiology, kinesiology, and sport science classes. I continued to experiment on myself to see what exercises resulted in the biggest gains, and got rid of others that didn't have a good "return on investment." My teammates and other athletes gave me a lot of resistance over the strength program that first year, but after most of the athletes saw the fruits of their iron-pressing labor, they all became convinced.

I know the personal experiences of one coach may not be enough to convince you to start incorporating weight training into your training program. That is why we will start off by going over current and past research on strength training with cyclists and endurance performance.

After going through past and current research, we will discuss how to incorporate strength training into your own training plan. This will include the concept of periodization in planning out your yearly plan, where strength training fits in, and how to maintain strength throughout the season for general health and performance.

We will then go over the nuts and bolts of the program. For this section, we'll cover how many days a week to exercise, what sets and reps to use, how to determine the appropriate weights to start with, how to warm-up for weight workouts, and how often to change up the movements and exercises. We will also delve into pre-and post-workout nutrition for your strength-training sessions. The nutritional needs of weight workouts vary quite a bit when compared to cycling workouts, and how we approach these workouts from a nutritional standpoint changes quite a bit as a result. We will also touch on the benefits of mobility work, such as foam rolling. And we'll discuss scientifically proven supplements that may also be beneficial.

Rest assured that this program has been designed to be very efficient. These are the movements and exercises that I have seen give the most "bang for your buck" in improving cycling performance. If you are looking for a program that will help you put on a lot of muscle mass, this is not your program. This program is all about increasing endurance performance and health. It is as much about your current cycling performance as it is about the "long game" and increasing quality of life.

The last part of this book will be an extensive library of movements, exercises, and mobility work, with detailed photos and descriptions. My goal is to give you an excellent resource to learn how to setup and execute these movements with a safe, powerful method.

In summary, I am excited to present you with a complete weight-training program to incorporate into your cycling to increase performance and stay injury-free, whether you are a weekend warrior, amateur racer, or aspiring professional.

Why Weight Train for Cycling?

Most professional cyclists don't appear as strong, beast-like individuals. They are thin, with sunken chests and scrawny arms. Not exactly the image of a typical strength athlete because they *aren't* the typical strength athlete. They have incredible lung capacity, efficient cardiovascular systems, and strong powerful legs. They also have to be able to produce forces with quick muscle contractions, not the typical slow contractions we see when doing a squat. So does this mean that strength training is not beneficial to the average cyclist? Hardly!

There are many reasons we are seeing more professional cyclists hit the gym in the off season and I would argue that those reasons are important for amateurs as well. We will go through the major benefits the gym can provide to cyclists both on and off the bike, but before we do, I want to correct a few common misconceptions. Strength does not equal size. As cyclists, our primary concern is strength-to-weight ratio. While some hypertrophy is needed to gain strength, better innervation of the motor units provides equal gains in strength. Lifting heavy weights is one of the best ways to improve innervation of muscles. It is also incredibly hard to gain muscle mass when lifting if you continue to ride your bike. Ultimately, if you want to get better at riding your bike, the solution is – you need to ride your bike! Weight training can be a very complementary ancillary task to cycling, but it does not replace the need to put in miles on the road.

A quick bit of information about this section before we dig into the science. As many of my athletes have told me, I tend to geek out on the science side of training. If this is not your thing, I would suggest skipping ahead to the conclusion portion of the following section for a quick synopsis of the studies. If it is your thing, dig in and enjoy as there are some very interesting studies being done on weight training with cyclists.

Force Production and Metabolic Improvements

How much force is needed in cycling? From power meter data, we can get very useful torque data to find the true forces needed in cycling. They aren't huge, but we need to reproduce them for a long time. If you are racing, you likely end your race with an explosive burst to the line. Torque and strength matter there. Going through data from professional to amateurs, we typically see peak torque values at 200%+ of body weight. If we are able to increase strength so that the athlete can produce higher peak torque levels, then riding at the reduced torque levels of cycling uses relatively less of our maximal strength, resulting in less fatigue. Furthermore, studies have shown that only force production declines with fatigue.

"This study examined EMG amplitude and frequency changes during a bout of fatiguing cycling. Trained cyclists (M = 11; F = 6) cycled for two hours at their ventilatory threshold (~66% VO2max), interspersed with five 1-minute sprints, followed by a 3-km time trial. EMGs of the vastus lateralis, vastus medialis, and rectus femoris were recorded for 30 seconds at 15, 75, and 115 minutes of cycling. Pedal frequency and oxygen consumption [VO2] were measured simultaneously. Maximal voluntary isometric strength was tested before and following cycling to indicate strength losses from fatigue. Maximum amplitude and average frequency for each pedal cycle were averaged for each 30-second measurement period.

Maximal voluntary isometric force declined by 21% after cycling, indicating fatigue. Pedal frequency did not change during the exercise. Rectus femoris EMG frequency decreased over time, which is to be expected with fatigue.

Implication. Contrary to expectations, only rectus femoris EMG frequency was altered with fatigue. There were no other amplitude or frequency changes in the quadriceps muscles in spite of significant fatigue."

Kremenic, I. J., Glace, B. W., & McHugh, M. P. (2008). **EMG changes during a prolonged bout of cycling.** *ACSM 55th Annual Meeting Indianapolis.* Presentation number 2501

If you are starting with a higher capacity to create force, the drop in force production from fatigue is significantly less. In fact, you are less likely to feel fatigue at all from the smaller force requirements of cycling as compared to that required in weight lifting. It is hard to create the amount of time under tension needed in cycling to drive these increases in force production. While some short, over-geared efforts are effective at creating the necessary torque, the dynamics of cycling make it hard to maintain that torque for very long.

It is also that time under tension that helps increase the innervation of muscle motor units in the legs. Stimulating more motor units is key to driving adaptation to strength training. Work done by Dr. Elwood Henneman (1964) has shown that muscles will fire smaller motor units first and progress to bigger fibers as force increases. This is important when looking at how best to improve muscle innervation and overall muscle adaptation. Movements that require less force will typically stimulate fewer muscle fibers resulting in more fatigue in those fibers. If we are able to make a better brain-to-muscle nerve connection and stimulate more motor units of the muscle, then we can effectively lengthen time to fatigue. To do that, we need to train our muscles at higher force levels than typically seen in cycling. I would even argue that this is a good indication that to maximize our gains in the gym, we need to lift items that are relatively heavy, at least heavier than most endurance athlete strength programs prescribe.

"A hypothesis is advanced that the interrelationships between the functional properties of motor units and the mitochondrial ATPase content of their fibers depend upon the size of the motor neurons which innervate them: the size of the cell dictates its excitability, its excitability determines the degree of use of the motor unit, and its "usage" in turn, specifies or influences the type of muscle fiber required. It is suggested that this size principle also governs the properties of gamma motor units."

ELWOOD HENNEMAN AND CAMILLE B. OLSON2 (1964) **RELATIONS BETWEEN STRUCTURE AND FUNCTION IN THE DESIGN OF SKELETAL MUSCLES** Department of Physiology, Harvard Medical School, Boston, Massachusetts

---

Additionally, it doesn't seem to matter what age or sex you are – voluntary contraction rates are similar for everyone. In a study done by Christie, A., & Kamen, G. (2009), **Gender and Age-Related Training Adaptations in Maximal Motor-Neuron Firing Rate**, they noted that, "Although older individuals and females had lower maximum voluntary contraction forces and lower maximum motor unit firing rates than young males, respectively, they showed similar adaptations in maximum voluntary contraction force and maximum motor unit firing rate in their response to training." These groups also increased force production without any significant changes in muscle size. Essentially, they were able to utilize more of the muscle, creating more force, without adding mass. Sounds ideal for a cyclist, where every gram matters.

"This study investigated potential age and gender differences in the training-related adaptations in muscular force and maximum motor unit firing rates. Young (M = 15; F = 15) and older (M = 15; F = 15) Ss completed two testing sessions, separated by two weeks. During each testing session measures of maximum voluntary contraction force of the dorsiflexors and maximum motor unit firing rates in the tibialis anterior were obtained. During the two-week interval between testing sessions, individuals in the control group were asked to carry out their normal daily activities, while individuals in the training group were asked to participate in a total of six isometric strength training sessions (three per week).

At baseline there were no differences in maximum voluntary contraction force or maximum firing rate between the training and control groups. However, also at baseline, maximum voluntary contraction force was lower in the older Ss when compared to the young and lower in females than in males. The trained group showed a significant 17.8% increase in maximum voluntary contraction force following training, while the control group showed little change (+2.2%)."

Christie, A., & Kamen, G. (2009). **Gender and age-related training adaptations in maximal moto-neuron firing rate**. *ACSM 56th Annual Meeting, Seattle, Washington.* Presentation number 2700.

The metabolic improvements of strength training have been a bit more controversial. There have been several studies showing no improvements of power at the lactate threshold, VO2, or in Wingate tests to assess anaerobic ability. However, most of those studies had some serious limitations with design and are not representative of how most athletes are integrating strength training into their cycling.

One recent study by Ronnestad, Hansen, Hollan, and Ellefsen (2015) investigated power output for two groups of cyclists, one doing just endurance training and the other endurance training plus heavy strength training. The study showed that the group doing heavy strength training plus endurance training showed better power improvements for 40k time trials, as well as better power in short Wingate tests.

"The purpose was to investigate the effect of 25 weeks heavy strength training in young elite cyclists. Nine cyclists performed endurance training and heavy strength training (ES) while seven cyclists performed endurance training only (E). ES, but not E, resulted in increases in isometric half squat performance, lean lower body mass, peak power output during Wingate test, peak aerobic power output (W_{max}), power output at 4 mmol L^{-1} [la^-], mean power output during 40-min all-out trial, and earlier occurrence of peak torque during the pedal stroke ($P < 0.05$). ES achieved superior improvements in W_{max} and mean power output during 40-min all-out trial compared with E ($P < 0.05$). The improvement in 40-min all-out performance was associated with the change toward achieving peak torque earlier in the pedal stroke ($r = 0.66$, $P < 0.01$). Neither of the groups displayed alterations in VO_{2max} or cycling economy. In conclusion, heavy strength training leads to improved cycling performance in elite cyclists as evidenced by a superior effect size of ES training vs E training on relative improvements in power output at 4 mmol L^{-1} [la^-], peak power output during 30-s Wingate test, W_{max}, and mean power output during 40-min all-out trial."

Ronnestad, B. R., Hansen, J., Hollan, I. and Ellefsen, S. (2015), **Strength training improves performance and pedaling characteristics in elite cyclists**. Scandinavian Journal of Medicine & Science in Sports, 25: e89–e98. doi: 10.1111/sms.12257

One other study that might help explain the results that Ronnestad, et al. found in their study was done by Porter, Reidy, Bhattari, and Rasmussen (2014). They found that 12 weeks of resistance exercise increased skeletal muscle mitochondria respiratory capacity and function. This would essentially allow the mitochondria, the energy factories of the cells, to process more nutrients to create fuel at a higher rate. In turn, this would let us increase the workload of the muscles or power on the bike, and may explain the results seen by Ronnestad, et al.

"Collectively, 12-weeks of resistance exercise training resulted in qualitative and quantitative changes in skeletal muscle mitochondrial respiration. This adaptation occurs with modest changes in mitochondrial proteins and transcript expression. Resistance exercise training appears to be a means to augment the respiratory capacity and intrinsic function of skeletal muscle mitochondria."

Porter C1, Reidy PT, Bhattarai N, Sidossis LS, Rasmussen BB. (2014), **Resistance Exercise Training Alters Mitochondrial Function in Human Skeletal Muscle**. Med Sci Sports Exerc. 2014 Dec 23.

Posture, Mobility, Weight Loss, and General Health Implications

Strength training is important not only for strength gains, but also for increasing effective joint ranges and mobility. The stronger we are, the better we can control extremities through a broader range of motion. One of the most challenging aspects of riding a bike efficiently is maintaining an ideal position. Most cyclists struggle with mobility and maintaining an effective hip range of motion while keeping a neutral spine on the bike. This is very evident when looking at a rider's position on a time trial or triathlon bike. Typical efficient aerodynamic positions require around 120 degrees of hip flexion, which can be trained in the weight room with squats where we are requiring the hips to drive power well past 120 degrees of flexion. An ideal road bike position typically requires ~110 degrees of hip flexion, which is still 20 degrees past where most people typically flex their hips. Training in a greater range of motion will result in better control in movements requiring less range of motion.

It should be noted that bike fit can accommodate virtually any hip range of motion. As a bike fitter, we often have to accommodate tight hamstrings, glutes, and other limitations, but those limitations sometimes don't result in an ideal position. It is an accommodated position that makes compromises to power production for better comfort for the rider. By working on mobility, both in and out of the weight room, we achieve a better, more efficient position.

It is also important to define what we mean by "core." We define core as the ability to maintain a neutral spine while extremities apply forces against resistance. Applying that to the bike helps maintain a neutral spine, or at a minimum lumbar spine, while the legs produce power. To do that we need good hip function and mobility, glute activation, and core strength. Studies have shown that the most effective core movements are squatting and deadlifting. Most people don't fail at front squatting from lack of leg strength; they fail due to lack of core strength.

There was an interesting study done looking at core strength and cycling performance. Researchers had a group of cyclists perform two performance tests, one rested and one after completing a core-fatiguing workout. In the second test after the core-fatiguing workout, leg forces remained unaltered but the researchers saw increased lateral and sagittal ranges of motion. Essentially they had less control of their hip, knee, and ankle joints, which could increase the potential of injury.

> "Core fatigue resulted in altered cycling mechanics that might increase the risk of injury because the knee joint is potentially exposed to greater stress. Improved core stability and endurance could promote greater alignment of the lower extremity when riding for extended durations as the core is more resistant to fatigue."
>
> Abt, John P.; Smoliga, James M.; Brick, Matthew J.; Jolly, John T.; Lephart, Scott M.; Fu, Freddie H. (2007), **Relationship Between Cycling Mechanics and Core Stability.** Journal of Strength & Conditioning Research: November 2007

The improved core strength and posture not only benefits cycling, but can also help overall well-being later in life. Strength training leads to better kinesthetic awareness, better core development, and better posture. Recently we have seen the connection between posture and hormonal response in people. It has been shown that standing upright in traditionally more powerful positions actually results in better testosterone, growth hormones, and other anabolic hormones, while reducing cortisol and other stress hormones. Essentially, having good posture can make you healthier inside and out.

"As predicted, high power posers performed better and were more likely to be chosen for hire, and this relationship was mediated only by presentation quality, not speech quality. Power pose condition had no effect on body posture during the social evaluation, thus highlighting the relationship between preparatory nonverbal behavior and subsequent performance."

Cuddy, Amy J.C., Caroline A. Wilmuth, and Dana R. Carney. **"The Benefit of Power Posing Before a High-Stakes Social Evaluation."** Harvard Business School Working Paper, No. 13-027, September 2012.

Weight Loss

There are many people who pick up the sport of cycling to lose weight and that is a great idea! Along with a good nutritional program, burning extra calories through a low impact activity like cycling can be a very useful tool in achieving a healthy weight. However, we can get a much higher metabolic response from weight lifting than from endurance exercise. Estimated post oxygen consumption (EPOC) after exercise can tell us how much the activity has increased our metabolic rate and for how long. This "after burn" can drastically impact our daily calorie expenditure and help us achieve the negative caloric balance needed to lose weight. Intensity influences EPOC more than duration (Bahr & Sejersted, 1991) which is why we typically see much higher levels post-resistance training versus what we see after endurance activities.

> "After exercise, there is an increase in O2 consumption termed the excess post exercise O2 consumption (EPOC). In this study, we have examined the effect of exercise intensity on the time course and magnitude of EPOC. Six healthy male subjects exercised on separate days for 80 minutes at 29%, 50%, and 75% of maximal O2 uptake (VO2max) on a cycle ergometer. O2 uptake, R value, and rectal temperature were measured while the subjects rested in bed for 14 hours post exercise, and the results were compared with those of an identical control experiment without exercise. An increase in O2 uptake lasting for 0.3 +/-0.1 hour (29% exercise), 3.3 +/-0.7 hour (50%) and 10.5 +/-1.6 hour (75%) was observed. EPOC was 1.3 +/-0.46 l(29%), 5.7 +/-1.7 l (50%), and 30.1 +/-6.4 l (75%). There was an exponential relationship between exercise intensity and total EPOC, both during the first 2 hours and the next 5 hours of recovery. Hence, prolonged exercise at intensities above 40% to 50% of VO2max is required in order to trigger the metabolic processes that are responsible for the prolonged EPOC component extending beyond 2 hours post exercise."
>
> Bahr R, Sejersted OM. (1991), **Effect of Intensity of Exercise on Excess Post Exercise O2 Consumption. Metabolism**. 1991 Aug; 40(8):836-41.

To further show the differences that exercise intensity has on post-oxygen consumption, Phelian et al. investigated the differences in EPOC of cycling at 75% of VO2 max and 50% VO2max when controlled by energy expenditure (Phelian, J.F, Reinke, E., Harris, M.A. and Melby, C.L. 1997. Post-exercise energy expenditure and substrate oxidation in young women resulting from exercise bouts of different intensity. Journal of the American College of Nutrition, 16(2), 140-146). VO2 Max is a term which means the maximum rate of oxygen consumption, which is measured during specific periods of exercise. Essentially, both groups kept pedaling until they had burned 500 calories, except one was riding at 75% of VO2max, while the other was only at 50% VO2max. The lower intensity group had to ride longer to burn those calories but ended up with a significantly lower EPOC level. If you want to burn more calories with your workouts, opt on the side of going harder versus easier and longer.

An interesting study done by Elliot, Diane L., Goldberg, Linn, Kuehl, and Kerry S. showed that heavy strength training results in 62% more EPOC than cycling at 80% of the max heart rate 30 minutes post-activity. Essentially, you are going to burn more energy post-exercise after strength training than you would after cycling. (Elliot, Diane L.; Goldberg, Linn; Kuehl, Kerry S., The Journal of Strength & Conditioning Research, May 1992)

"Training volume seemed to influence both EPOC magnitude and duration, whereas workload influenced mostly the magnitude. Short rest intervals (<60 s) increased the EPOC magnitude, but not the overall energy expenditure. Conclusion. Resistance training with high intensity and volume, performed with short rest intervals (as in circuit training), probably have greater impact on EPOC. Methodological procedures, particularly time of post-exercise observation and RMR assessment, should be standardized to an appropriate quantification of the actual influence of resistance training on EPOC."

Paulo Farinatti, Antonio Gil Castinheiras Neto, and Nádia Lima da Silva, **"Influence of Resistance Training Variables on Excess Postexercise Oxygen Consumption: A Systematic Review,"** ISRN Physiology, vol. 2013, Article ID 825026, 10 pages, 2013. doi:10.1155/2013/825026

Another study by Osterberg, K. L. & Melby, C. L showed that EPOC and resting metabolic rate were at 4.2% higher 16 hours following strength training. While the overall calorie expenditures post exercise are relatively small, their cumulative effect can be quite large over time.

"This study determined the effect of an intense bout of resistive exercise on postexercise oxygen consumption, resting metabolic rate, and resting fat oxidation in young women (N=7, ages 22-35). On the morning of Day 1, resting metabolic rate (RMR) was measured by indirect calorimetry. At 13:00 hr., preexercise resting oxygen consumption was measured followed by 100 min of resistive exercise. Postexercise oxygen consumption was then measured for a 3-hr recovery period. On the following morning (Day 2), RMR was once again measured in a fasted state at 07:00. Postexercise oxygen consumption remained elevated during the entire 3-hr postexercise recovery period compared to the pre-exercise baseline. Resting metabolic rate was increased by 4.2% (p<.05) from Day 1 (morning prior to exercise: 1,419 +/-58 kcal/24hr) compared to Day 2 (16 hr. following exercise: 1,479 +/-kcal/24hr). Resting fat oxidation as determined by the respiratory exchange ratio was also significantly elevated on Day 2 compared to Day 1. These results indicate that among young women, acute strenuous resistance exercise of the nature used in this study is capable of producing modest but prolonged elevations of postexercise metabolic rate and possibly fat oxidation."

Osterberg KL, & Melby CL. **Effect of Acute Resistance exercise on Postexercise Oxygen Consumption and Resting Metabolic Rate in Young Women**. Int J Sport Nutr Exerc Metab. 2000 Mar;10(1):71-81.

Anecdotally, I typically see more weight loss in athletes doing strength training, or strength and endurance training, than athletes just doing endurance training alone. This difference is higher in women than in men, but both tend to see more weight loss when strength training is included in their training. The increased muscle mass (which increases resting metabolic rate), EPOC, and lack of a strong hunger drive post-exercise all tend to lead to a negative caloric balance when following a sensible diet.

Preventing Muscle Loss

Sarcopenia is the gradual loss of muscle mass and function with aging. It primarily affects people over the age of 30, with many sedentary individuals losing 3-5% of their muscle mass per decade. The loss of muscle mass also affects metabolism and finding a healthy body weight since maintaining muscle mass costs calories. As noted above, this increases basal metabolic rate, or the amount of calories you burn per day just by living. Sarcopenia is often thought to be part of the cause for body fat gain later in life. Having more muscle mass and function later in life directly impacts quality of life in our later years as well.

Cycling alone won't help maintain that mass. While endurance exercise is beneficial in the elderly who are already experiencing the effects of sarcopenia, it doesn't provide enough resistance to prevent muscle loss as we age. We need to provide higher levels of resistance to stress the musculature system to maintain mass and function. The good thing is that several studies have shown that moderate strength training can prevent sarcopenia from occurring.

Bone Density

One other aspect of general health that cycling doesn't help with is bone strength. Since cycling is not weight bearing, and ideally isn't an impact sport, it doesn't stress the skeletal system enough for the bones to strengthen. In fact, there have been a few elite level cyclists who retired fairly early in their careers due to early onset of osteopenia. The most well-known of these athletes is Chris Boardman. In an interview done in the UK's Daily Mail, Boardman stated that, "I had to give up cycling at the age of 32 because I had the bones of an old woman." While Boardman had a family history of osteoporosis, 32 is still a very early age to have to retire from a sport where he was very successful in the past.

A study done by Nichols, Palmer, and Levy (2003) with highly trained master cyclists showed that the cyclists had lower bone mass than non-athletes. This is an interesting study because the cyclists who had been training or racing for at least 10 years had lower bone mass than non-athletes of the same age and body weight of non-athletes. This may be from a theorized dermal calcium loss during exercise. Essentially muscle contractions use calcium to both contract and release the muscle. During extensive endurance exercise, it is theorized that if calcium stores become low, the body may "steal" calcium from the skeletal system. While the exact mechanism is still a bit unclear, we do know that endurance exercise does lead to mineral loss in sweat, which may over time reduce the overall mineral content of the bones.

"BMD (measured by DXA) of the spine (L2-L4) and total hip was significantly ($P<0.033$) lower in the master cyclists compared to both age-matched controls and young adult cyclists. Total body BMD was lower in the master cyclists compared to the young-adults ($P<0.033$). Furthermore, four (15%) of the master cyclists, but none of the men in the other groups, had T-scores (spine and/or hip) lower than-2.5. Weight-bearing exercise performed during teen and young adult years did not appear to influence BMD, as there were no differences at any site between those within the upper and lower 50th percentiles for weight-bearing exercise during the 12-18, 19-34, or 35-49 year time periods. These data indicate that master cyclists with a long history of training exclusively in cycling have low BMD compared to their age-matched peers. Although highly trained and physically fit, these athletes may be at high risk for developing osteoporosis with advancing age."

Nichols JF, Palmer JE, Levy SS. (2003), **Low Bone Mineral Density in Highly Trained Male Master Cyclists.** Osteoporosis Int. 2003 Aug; 14(8):644-9. Epub 2003 Jul 11.

While some studies have shown that mountain biking may be better than road cycling in maintaining bone mass, mountain biking alone only puts the cyclists on a par with other sedentary individuals. (Warner SE, Shaw JM, Dalsky GP. (2002), **Bone Mineral Density of Competitive Male Mountain and Road Cyclists.** *Bone* 30(1):281-6.)

Science has also shown us that osteopenia, low bone mineral density, is relatively easy to prevent. Just do weight-bearing exercise with strength training. This produces the best results. While the exact protocol is quite varied in the studies, most results have shown that as little as 1-2 weight-training sessions a week can have a very positive effect on bone health in both men and women.

"Effects of exercise varied greatly among studies, with six interventions having a positive effect on BMD and two interventions having no significant effect. It appears that resistance training alone or in combination with impact-loading activities are most osteogenic for this population, whereas the walking trials had limited effect on BMD. Therefore, regular resistance training and impact-loading activities should be considered as a strategy to prevent osteoporosis in middle-aged and older men. High quality randomized controlled trials are needed to establish the optimal exercise prescription."

Bolam KA, van Uffelen JG, Taaffe DR. 2013. **The Effect of Physical Exercise on Bone Density in Middle-aged and Older Men: a Systematic Review**. Osteoporosis Int. 2013 Nov;24(11):2749-62. Doi: 10.1007/s00198-013-2346-1. Epub 2013 Apr 4.

Conclusion

I think the evidence is pretty clear. Strength training can not only increase your performance on the bike through potentially increasing force production, skeletal muscular respiration, and nerve function, but it can also help with general health, both now and later in life. Sarcopenia and osteopenia are both real risks for cyclists and should be a consideration when designing your training plan. In terms of performance, we have to be careful about how we program our workouts and make sure the weight training isn't impacting the on-the-bike training significantly. Good workout programming should incorporate fatigue management and maintain good recovery protocol to make the most of your time on the bike and in the weight room. One of the most important takeaways from a lot of the studies on both of those diseases is that they can be preventable with as little as one strength-training session per week. Even a competitive cyclist in the middle of race season can find a way to include a short weight training session in their training plan.

One other important takeaway from the studies is that heavier lifting tends to have favorable results in both performance and health. While doing strength workouts with relatively lighter weights is needed at times, picking up the bigger weights and doing a few less reps will have a much bigger impact on your fitness and overall health. This does put a bigger load on the central nervous system and the risk of injury is slightly higher, but prioritizing these workouts before hopping on the bike is crucial for safety and maximizing performance.

In the next section we will walk through how to program your workouts around your cycling as well as alternating nutrition, including good recovery hygiene, and maximizing your programing to make you the best cyclist you can be.

How to Lift

If you made it through all that science talk, you are probably wondering, "Now what do I do?" And that is a valid question since there are several methods, styles, and programs used in those studies with a variety of results. Fortunately for us, there are some commonalities in the studies that would be good for us to mimic.

First off, lift heavy! There was a pretty strong correlation in most of the studies that lifting with less reps and more weight resulted in better outcomes in both general health markers and in performance of athletes. This is counter to what is often recommended for endurance athletes. Many endurance-athlete weight-training programs recommend lighter weights with higher reps. While this can help with some general conditioning, it does not optimize your time in the gym to get the best results possible.

Second, for performance benefits, use a periodized system to change the focus of your lifting. Periodization of training is a concept originally created by Hans Seyle to systematically plan out training to reach peak performance. It is based on the biological response to stress and adaptation. Essentially, lifting the same amount all year long will result in a stagnation of progress and performance. Phases of lifting must be used to correspond to different times of the year to maximize gains and performance on the bike. Typically we would divide a strength program into a transition, base, hypertrophy, and explosive phases.

Third, explosive movements should be used to maximize the neurological benefits of lifting and increase cycling performance. An example of an explosive movement would be squatting down slowly, then exploding into a jump. This movement mimics the quicker muscle contraction needed on the bike to transfer the increased strength and force production into power (force multiplied by pedal velocity) on the bike.

Additionally, here are some other key points from successful lifting programs:

- Strength training frequency should be between 1-3 days a week, with two days a week showing the most benefit for time invested.
- Length of workouts should range between 30-45 minutes, not including any warm-ups or specific mobility work.
- For most movements, 3-5 sets done with 3-7 reps is ideal for strength building; 2-3 sets with 3-5 movements works for explosive movements.
- Weight should be between 70-85% of one-rep max for strength building, and 50-60% of one-rep max or bodyweight for explosive movements.
- Lifting velocity should be controlled for heavier movements, and controlled eccentric movements with fast concentric movements for explosive movements.
- Rest intervals should be standardized to get an honest assessment on improvements. Most rest intervals should be 1-2 minutes. Explosive movements need a longer recovery period between sets.
- Full body workouts tend to be more beneficial for endurance athletes than splitting up upper and lower bodies. Plus, they are more efficient, allowing for less time in the gym and more time on the bike.

All the workouts in this book will adhere to the principles described above and are designed to be as efficient and optimized as possible. They will help you gain strength, improve general health, and improve cardiovascular endurance to improve performance on the bike.

How to Use the Programs in this Book

Most cyclists who are training to improve cycling performance will follow a typical "season" pattern. They take a bit of time off in the fall, start back with some base training over the winter, progressing to more intensity as they get closer to the spring and races or events. Weight training should also progress in a similar way, through a periodized program that matches the training being done on the bike.

It is important to realize that you can't just jump into any program in this book and expect good results and not put yourself at risk for injury. There is a specific progression to the programs in this book and one builds upon the other. They are designed to go from an adaptation phase during the transition time of your cycling year, to a strength phase during the base-building of your year, to an explosive phase as you get closer to competitive events, to a maintenance phase through the racing/riding season.

That doesn't necessarily mean you can't start a strengthening program in the middle of the season. It just means you have to be safe, expect a slightly longer transition time, and respect the additional recovery time needed.

Phases of Weight Training

- **Transition:** This is the time of year when we allow for a bit more recovery from all of our training and focus on developing skills. Becoming very comfortable with all the weight training movements during this time of the year is critical for a successful and safe weight-training program for the rest of the year. We recommend starting each weight-training workout with some skills work at this time of the year. Using light weight, working through a good squat pattern or deadlift form can make a huge difference later in the year when we move on to heavier weights. This is also a good time of the year to allow the body to start to adapt to the different demands placed on it in the weight room. It isn't uncommon to end up with a bit of delayed onset muscle soreness after a few easy weight sessions, and this time of year allows us to focus a bit more on systemic recovery and to respect the physiological adaptation phase of the body. This phase is primarily made up of 3-5 sets with 8-12 reps at moderately light weight.

- **Strength:** This is the "meat and potatoes" time of the year. This phase builds on the skills and early adaptations gained during the transition period and starts to put an emphasis on increasing max strength. The main reason we are heading to the gym is to get strong, and there isn't a better way to do that than by lifting heavy weights. The heavier weights drive a higher neurological adaptation as well as optimize our time in the gym. This phase of lifting is typically done with lower reps and a moderate number of sets, and utilizes complex multi-joint movements such as front squats, deadlifts, bench presses, and pull-ups.

- **Explosive/Plyometric:** After building strength, we want to transform that into explosive power to become more useful on the bike. After all, pedaling your bike slowly with a lot of torque isn't an ideal way to ride a bike. To help build leg speed and make the strength gains made in the gym a bit more applicable, we utilize explosive movements and plyometrics to make improvements to muscle contraction speed. Plyometrics are essentially quick movements with maximal muscle contractions such as jumping, sprinting on the bike, or other quick accelerations. This phase features 2-3 sets with 4-8 reps for most movements.

- **In-Season:** Typically, during the race season or the time of the year when you are cycling at a higher volume, it is beneficial to reduce the time spent in the gym in favor of more time on the bike. For most, this time of the year coincides with the summer when the weather is better and we would want to spend more time on the bike anyways. It is important to keep at least one day a week in the weight room to maintain the strength gains. 1-2 sets with 8-10 reps of all movements is recommended for this phase. This workout shouldn't impair other cycling workouts if added into the training schedule on appropriate days. It is not recommend to do any strength workouts within 72 hours of a race or event.

Rules for Implementing Weight Lifting into Your Cycling Training

How we incorporate the weights into a typical cycling-training program will vary a bit according to the time of year, your goals, and your individualized recovery rate. If your goals include being able to crush the local Saturday Morning Worlds group ride, then you'd want to make sure you aren't lifting weights on Friday. This is also true for key workouts such as interval work or bigger volume days. The weight training should complement the cycling workouts, not impair them. Even though there are a lot of individualized factors here, there are some common rules that will help you:

- Even though this sounds counter-intuitive, you should do your weight workouts on your harder riding days of the week. This will allow you to consolidate the harder workouts in your schedule on the same day and preserve the easier recovery days in your weekly schedule as well.
- Listen to your body and lift easier if you are fatigued. When we are tired we start to see form deteriorate and the potential for injury rise. This bears repeating; our first priority in the gym is safety. Lifting heavy weights when tired is not only less effective, it isn't safe. Take an extra day to recover and get under the barbell the next day.
- Lift before you ride. Along the same lines as the previous rule, when lifting weights we will want to be recovered as much as possible to maintain proper form. Many of the complex multi-joint movements require a high amount of neurological functioning which is often impaired after endurance training. Be safe and lift the iron after you ride your bike.
- If possible, don't lift in the morning, or at least within the first hour after waking up. I know, I know...it is often the easiest time of the day to fit this in, especially when trying to adhere to the previous rule of lifting before you ride. But the risk of injury, specifically spine injuries, is quite a bit higher in the morning due to the swelling of spinal discs as we sleep. Spinal discs go through a process of rehydrating when sleeping, and dehydrating throughout the day. It is this change in hydration that accounts for our change in height during the day. We are typically slightly taller in the morning and shorter in the evening. Think of a fully hydrated spinal disc as a water balloon. When they are full, they are more likely to burst with compression. When only half full they can adapt to compressive loads. The same holds true for our vertebral discs. Protect your back and wake up an hour earlier if you want to do your strength work in the morning.
- Finally, prioritize your cycling workouts. Weight lifting is an ancillary movement. We are doing it to improve our performance on the bike. The rule of specificity states that training that matches the demands of our key events is the most effective. In our case, that event is cycling, and weight training alone will not make you fast on the bike. You have to ride your bike to be fast. Weight training should complement your riding and not replace it. If you have to choose between the two, ride your bike.

Weekly Samples of how to Mix Weight Training and Cycling

Example one: 5 days a week riding, 2 days weight training in a typical base phase:

Monday	Tuesday	Wednesday	Thursday	Friday	Saturday	Sunday
Rest	Endurance Day. 2 hours	Threshold Intervals 2 x 20 minutes. 2 Hours	High Cadence. 2 Hours	Rest Day	Threshold Intervals or Group Ride. 2-3 hours	Long Endurance Day. 4 Hours.
		Weight Training. 1 hour			Weight Training. 1 hour	

Example two: 5 days a week cycling, 3 days weight training in typical base phase:

Monday	Tuesday	Wednesday	Thursday	Friday	Saturday	Sunday
Rest	Threshold Intervals 2 x 20 minutes. 2 Hours	High Cadence. 1.5 Hours	Endurance. 2 Hours	Rest Day	Threshold Intervals or Group Ride. 2 – 3 hours	Long Endurance Day. 4 Hours.
	Weight Training. 1 hour		Weight Training. 1 hour		Weight Training. 1 hour	

Example three: 5 days a week cycling, 3 days weight training in a build/pre-season phase:

Monday	Tuesday	Wednesday	Thursday	Friday	Saturday	Sunday
Rest	Interval day. 2 Hours	Endurance day. 2 Hours	Sprint Work. 2 hours	Rest Day	Group Ride. 2 – 3 hours	Long Endurance Day. 4 Hours
	Weight Training. 1 hour		Plyometric, explosive training. 1 hour.		Weight Training. 1 hour	

Example four: 5 days a week cycling, 1 day weight training in race season:

Monday	Tuesday	Wednesday	Thursday	Friday	Saturday	Sunday
Rest	Interval day. 2 Hours	Endurance day. 2 Hours	Short Sprint Work. 1.5 hours	Rest Day	Pre-Race Openers. 1 Hour	Race. 3 Hours
	Weight Training. 45 minutes.		Plyometric, explosive training. 30 minutes			

*All strength workouts should include mobility work prior to training.
This will be detailed in the next section of the book.

Weight Training Terminology

Definitions

If you are new to the weight-training world, then you are probably wondering exactly what all these terms mean. Having a solid understanding of the terminology is critical to being able to follow the programs presented in this book.

- **Sets** – Performing one specific exercise for a specific number of repetitions or time without rest. In this book, all of the programs will have between 1-5 sets.
- **Reps or repetitions** – This is the specific number of times you perform a specific movement in one set. In this book, the programs will range between 3-15 reps. It is important to note that as the reps become lower, the amount of weight you can lift increases. You can lift more weight if you are only lifting it a few times.
- **1RM or one-rep max** – This is how much force, or weight an athlete can lift, for one repetition. This is important because we will use percentages of one rep max to prescribe intensity. For example, doing front squats for 5 sets at 5 reps at 75%1RM would be harder than front squats for 5 sets of 5 reps at 50%1RM.

  - o Doing a test for 1RM is hard, and can be dangerous. That is why we don't recommend specifically testing for your 1RM on each exercise. It is much safer and still just as accurate to use an equation to determine 1RM. In fact, several sports scientists have worked and continued to refine the equation used to predict 1RM based on the amount of weight you lift for a set number of repetitions. Specifically, the Bryzycki Formula has been tested and shown to be valid when using weight that results in the 7-10 repetition range.
  - o The Bryzycki formula is specifically: 1RM = (Weight Used) x 36 / (37 – Number of Reps) and this is what we recommend for determining 1RM.

- **Tempo** – This is how quickly you would lift the weight. At times we are performing exercises with more of an explosive movement, while at other times we perform the movement with a lot of control, holding weight at a specific point. Knowing how fast to perform the exercise is critical in being able to adhere to the exercise program as written.
- **Rest Period** – This is the amount of time to spend recovering between sets during a workout. This is closely related to the amount of sets and reps we are doing as well. Exercises done at lower reps and higher intensity often require more rest time between sets, while exercises done at higher reps with less intensity often need a bit less rest. Movements also done at a quicker tempo often require a bit more rest between sets.

- **Concentric Movement** – When performing an exercise, the primary working muscle contracts, or shortens to create a movement. This is considered a concentric movement because the muscle length is contracting, or shortening in length. For example, returning to standing from a squatting position is a concentric movement because the movement is created by muscles contracting.
- **Eccentric Movement** – This is the opposite of a concentric movement. Controlling the lengthening of a muscle is called an eccentric movement. An example of this would be lowering into a squat position from a standing position. This is done by muscles contracting slightly to control their lengthening and slowing the downward movement of the body.

  o Why is knowing what Concentric and Eccentric movements are important? Cycling is only a concentric movement. Our legs don't have to control the lengthening of the muscles in the pedal stroke, they only contract. For this reason, controlling tempo on the concentric movements is very important. Depending on the phase of the weight-training program, we may want to emphasize slower, more controlled movements to maximize time under tension, while at other times we may emphasize explosive movements to maximize power creation on the bike. Regardless of how we control tempo on the concentric portion of the movement, the eccentric portion of the movement is always done in a controlled manner. We don't want to drop weight quickly since that can drastically increase the risk of injury.

Warm Up

Why warm-up? Why don't we just jump into the gym and get under the barbell right away? We don't do that because our body needs to go through a physiological preparation before it can work optimally and prevent injuries. Essentially, warming up increases muscle temperature which increases the ability to contract, to become more elastic, and to relax fully. Warm joints will also increase mobility by increasing the production of synovial fluid, the lubrication of our joints. The cardio vascular system also adapts by dilating blood vessels to ease the flow of blood and to reduce the relative workload on the heart. The temperature of the blood also increases, which weakens the bond of oxygen to hemoglobin, and allows easier uptake by the muscles. Hormonally, we see changes that allow the body to utilize more carbohydrates and fats for energy, thus increasing endurance. Finally, following a good warm-up routine can increase adrenalin and help an athlete mentally prepare for the challenges of the workout.

For weight training there are two types of recommended warm-ups:

- **General Warm-Up:** This is essentially movement to gradually increase the body temperature and begin the beneficial hormonal changes. For cyclists, the best activity for this is cycling. This can be on a spin bike in the gym or an easy short ride. If on a spin bike, 5-15 minutes of easy endurance pace spinning, with a few short 10-15 seconds quick accelerations, is typically enough for most athletes to get a good sweat going. If riding outside, anywhere from 10-15 minutes typically works well. Riding from home to the gym is a great way to get in this general warm-up. The ride home also works as a good cool down. Ideally, the time between your general warm-up and workout should be less than 15 minutes.
- **Specific Warm-Up Sets:** Once you have finished your general warm-up, you will want to start most of the weight exercises with a few warm-up sets. These are essentially lightweight or bodyweight movements to prepare the specific muscles and joints used in the exercise. These should be done prior to your first work set (that is prescribed in the workouts) to allow you to be confident in the movement pattern and mentally prepare for the heavier sets to come. It is important that these are done so they don't create unnecessary fatigue. The following recommendations demonstrate how to incorporate warm-up sets into your workout:

  o Start with one set of ten movements at bodyweight or very light resistance. For example, when warming up for front squats this may be 10 bodyweight squats or just using the barbell.
  o The second set should be eight reps done at 50-55% of the weight you will use for your first work set. If your first work set for front squats is 100 pounds, then this set should be 50-55 pounds for eight reps.

o The last warm-up set should be three reps at 80-85% of your first work set. Again, as in our front squat example where we will be doing the first set at 100 pounds, this would be 80-85 pounds for three reps. After this you will be optimally prepared to complete that first work set.

o You should be following this protocol before most movements.

- **Mobility Work:** We will go into more detail in the foam rolling section, but between your general warm-up and specific warm-up sets would be a good time to add in specific mobility work. This may include area foam rolling, lacrosse ball work, or other techniques to increase functional range of motion. We don't recommend including static stretching during this time. Research has shown that static stretching before exercise will reduce performance and may potentially lead to more injuries.

Cool Downs

A light cool down can be very helpful in reducing recovery time. Some light movement allows the body to flush waste materials from muscles, allows the body to slowly decrease temperature and redistribute blood throughout the body, all of which can drastically help reduce recovery time. This can be another 5-10 minutes on a spin bike, 5-10 minutes on a foam roller (more to come on this), or that easy ride home after the gym. During this time you should also be starting to restore hydration by drinking fluids with added electrolytes.

Breathing

You wouldn't think explaining how to breathe would be something we need to do given that we all have survived this long. But proper breathing technique will not only increase performance, it is also a lot safer. Most athletes tend to hold their breath when lifting weights. This can lead to dangerous increases in blood pressure, light headedness, and eventually loss of consciousness. All of those videos on your tube showing a guy lifting weight, then losing consciousness and collapsing is from this increase in blood pressure. Following a proper breathing technique can also greatly decrease the risk of hernia.

The first step to improving your breathing is to be conscious of your breathing, especially during hard efforts. Gasping and panting like a doggie will just hyperventilate you and will not provide maximum oxygen to the blood, nor remove as much CO_2. You want to strive for controlled deep breaths with strong exhalations. If you concentrate on breathing out forcefully you will get rid of more CO_2 and your body will naturally bring in more oxygen as well.

Once you feel comfortable controlling your breathing while doing hard efforts, the next step to improving your respiration is to concentrate on belly breathing. In yoga, this is also called low breathing, and is also referred to as diaphragmatic breathing or abdominal breathing. This is basically breathing by expanding your belly on inhalation and contracting on exhalation. The primary advantage of this is that more air is taken in when inhaling due to increased movement of the lungs and the fact that the lower lobes of the lungs have a larger capacity than the upper lobes. During weight training you will want to inhale when you are lowering the weight or through the eccentric phase, and breathe out while pushing the weight up or during the concentric phase.

I found it easier to begin belly breathing by practicing at rest before learning how to use it while exercising. Practicing belly breathing also can help you relax and provide a general sense of well-being. Both are very good methods for recovery.

Belly Breathing Practice

1. Start by lying on your back on a comfortable surface with your knees bent, feet flat on the floor.
2. Place both hands on your belly, one on top of the other, just above your belly button.
3. Inhale deeply, trying to push your hands as high as possible. If you find it hard to raise your hands very much, try applying light pressure with your hands to provide a little extra resistance for your diaphragm to push against.
4. Hold for a second and exhale forcefully, letting your hands naturally drop. Try to pull your belly button to your spine but don't push your hands down to exhale.
5. Once you're comfortable doing this lying down, practice it in a sitting position, keeping your back straight, shoulders back.
6. When you are comfortable in the sitting position, start working on this breathing technique while training. With practice, it will start to become second nature while weight training and while riding your bike.

Nutrition

Nutrition is critical in making gains in the gym. While a good nutritional program can maximize gains from your time in the gym, a nutritional program that doesn't meet your physiological needs can prevent gains and even make you lose a bit of fitness from under-recovering from workouts. Both pre-workout and post-workout meals are important in optimizing gains, energy levels, and recovery, all the way down to a cellular level. While your overall nutritional program is just as important as your workout nutrition, covering general nutrition is a bit outside the scope of this book. Generally speaking, prioritizing whole, real foods while limiting processed foods is a very good place to start. To read more on general nutrition for athletes I would suggest going to the Precision Nutrition website at www.precisionnutrition.com.

Pre-Workout Meal

You will want to eat your pre-workout meal at least 1-2 hours prior to your workout to allow time for food to digest. The goals of the pre-workout meal are to have enough energy to make it through the workout, to increase hydration, boost performance, and preserve muscle mass. Specifically we want to make sure there are some carbohydrates for energy, and protein to prevent any catabolism (using muscles as energy) during the workout. Protein is very important in your pre-workout meal because it kick-starts the recovery process. Proteins are broken down into amino acids which are the foundation of several processes in the body that are required for recovery from hard workouts. Having circulating amino acids in your bloodstream has also been shown to reduce the amount of muscle damage markers such as creatine kinase and myoglobin. Preventing damage to your muscles while working out will have a huge impact on how quickly you recover post workout.

Carbohydrates are needed before exercise to provide glycogen, the fuel used by muscles. Carbohydrates also cause an insulin response which can be beneficial while exercising by preserving protein breakdown and increasing protein synthesis. Both of these processes will not only help with performance, but will help repair muscle as well. We tend to favor complex carbohydrates eaten an hour or two before exercise versus sugary sources closer to the workout to prevent potential digestive problems and for general health benefits.

While your pre-workout meal may also include fat, most fats haven't been shown to be beneficial or detrimental if eaten in moderation. The one exception to this is coconut oil or medium chain triglycerides which can act more as a carbohydrate and be broken down quickly enough to fuel muscles. All other fats in your pre-workout meal may slow digestion which can be problematic if you are eating closer than 2 hours before a workout. Fats are healthy and required in a balanced diet, just not in those hours right before a workout.

A couple of examples of good pre-workout meals:

- Whole fat plain Greek yogurt with vanilla protein powder and granola. 540 calories, 36grams of carbohydrates, 39grams of protein, and 28 grams of fat.
- Chicken breast, ½ cup sweet potato. 396 calories, 17 grams of carbohydrates, 55 grams of protein, and 10 grams of fat.
- Three large scrambled eggs, ½ cup sweet potato, and 1 table spoon-grated parmesan cheese. 412 calories, 19 grams of carbohydrates, 23 grams of protein, and 26 grams of fat.

During Workouts

During your strength workouts, the primary goals of anything you consume is to maintain hydration and circulating amino acids. Since most of our amino acids come from the digestion of protein, and protein takes at least 60 minutes to start to break down, consuming an amino acid supplement during or right before your weight workout can be very beneficial. We recommend finding a branch chain amino acid (BCAA) from a reputable supplement company. They can be in capsule or powdered form. Having it in powdered form makes it very easy to mix in your water bottle while in the gym. A good example would be the Amino Complex product from ThorneFX.

Post-Workout Meal

Our post-exercise needs are primarily hydration to restore cell function, refuel muscle and liver glycogen stores, rebuild damaged muscle cells, and maintain general nutrition. Unless you are doing two workouts on the same day, having any specific sport recovery products aren't really needed. Current research even shows that some of the quick digesting proteins in recovery drinks actually get digested too fast. They are in and out of our system too quickly to be beneficial. It also important to note that if you had a good pre-workout meal then the proteins from that meal are still circulating in your bloodstream after a workout. In this case, eating quick-digesting protein immediately after exercise wouldn't be beneficial.

Your post workout meal will probably not look a whole lot different than your pre-workout meal. If you ate a larger pre-workout meal, then you won't need a huge post-workout meal. The reverse of that is also true where you should have more nutrition post-workout if you had a smaller pre-workout meal. The post-workout meal should be made up of real foods and have a mix of carbohydrates, proteins, and fats. Carbohydrates are needed to restore glycogen levels in your muscles and liver. Protein provides additional amino acids to continue muscle repair and synthesis. Fats provide many required fat soluble vitamins that are needed for maximizing recovery.

A couple of examples of good post-workout meals:

- 8oz grass-fed steak, two cups grilled veggies, ½ cup brown rice. 356 calories, 42 grams of carbohydrates, 57 grams of protein, and 19 grams of fat.
- Protein smoothie with one scoop vanilla protein, one cup spinach, one cup frozen berries, and one cup unsweetened vanilla almond milk. 267 calories, 30 grams of carbohydrates, 19 grams of protein, and 10 grams of fat.

Supplements

Walk into any vitamin store or sports nutrition place these days and you will see a ridiculous number of products being sold to help build muscles, increase performance, reduce fatigue, lose weight, or improve recovery. Most don't have any scientific backing or are only supported by self-funded studies to show any reported benefits. The list of scientifically-supported products is actually quite short. From that list, here are the ones I have found to be the most effective for endurance athletes. You should consult your doctor if you have any health issues where supplements may be counter-indicated.

- **Creatine.** Creatine is probably the most well researched supplement on the market. Several studies have been done in both animal populations and in human trials, with favorable results in both increasing cognitive abilities and sports performance. These studies have also shown creatine to be safe. Creatine works by increasing the amount of energy available in the phosphocreatine energy system of the muscles. Essentially this allows the athlete to perform 1-2 more reps in the gym and over time that will result in bigger strength gains. Recent studies have shown creatine to be beneficial in reducing cortisol, the stress hormone, and increasing testosterone. Both of those changes would lead to better recovery, health, and overall sports performance (http://www.sciencedirect.com/science/article/pii/S0765159715000039). Our recommended dose is 5g per day, preferably in the morning.
- **Beet Juice.** Beet juice, or more accurately, the naturally occurring nitrates found in beet juice, work as a vasodilator in the body, helping increase the flow of blood throughout the vascular system. In cyclists, this has been shown to increase power output at the same oxygen consumption. Essentially this increases efficiency and reduces the consumption of oxygen at any given intensity level. In a study done by Dr. Andrew Jones at the University of Exeter, cyclists were able to ride 16.1km on average of 45 seconds after the ingestion of 500ml of beet juice. The same gains seen on the road can result in a slightly higher workload in the gym and better recovery post-workout. Science has shown that 500ml works well for most athletes, but we suggest experimenting a bit with dosing to see what works best for you. It is important to note that conversion of nitrate to nitric oxide is reliant on the bacteria in your mouth and stomach. For maximum effect, it is recommended that you avoid brushing your teeth or using mouthwash close to consuming beet juice.
- **L-Arginine.** L-Arginine is an amino acid that works very similarly to beet juice. It is a biological processor to nitric oxide in the body and can help to optimally dilate blood vessels to increase blood flow to working muscles and organs. There is also some evidence that shows that L-Arginine can also help support endocrine function and regulate insulin, glucagon, neurotransmitters, and growth hormone. The optimal dosage is 2-3 grams 45 minutes before working out. L-Arginine would take the place of beet juice and you should not take both together.

- **Amino Acids.** The protein we eat is broken down in the digestive tract to smaller units called amino acids. Nine are essential, meaning that we need to consume them in our diet, while another 7 are conditionally essential, meaning that our bodies can create them from other amino acids in normal conditions. Amino acids are the building blocks of cells in our bodies and are essential to recovery and energy levels. At any given time, we should have 100 grams of amino acids circulating in our blood stream, but through exercise, inadequate protein intake, or other illnesses that pool can become depleted. Since having adequate amino acids can also prevent the body from catabolizing skeletal muscle, it is important to keep these levels high while doing strength training. This is the main reason we advise getting some protein during your pre-and post-workout meals. But if you are a bit low on protein intake or it isn't convenient to eat a good protein source before your workout, such as in early morning workouts, it can be helpful to use a good amino acid supplement to ensure higher levels of muscle synthesis and repair. Five grams is a good place to start before workouts, but many athletes feel better with doses in the 8-10 gram range. Our suggestion for specific products is either ThorneFX's Amino Complex or Master Amino Pattern capsules by the International Nutrition Research Center.
- **Fish Oil.** There are several studies showing that fish oils can help protect against cardiovascular disease (http://www.ncbi.nlm.nih.gov/pubmed/18982874) and reduce asthma (http://www.ncbi.nlm.nih.gov/pubmed/16424411) primarily due to its anti-inflammatory effects in the body. Reducing inflammation is also crucial for repair in the body, including repairing the micro trauma created by weight training. Tendinosis and sore muscles are examples of inflammation in the body. We are constantly fighting inflammation in our body and fish oil can be extremely helpful in this battle. The omega-3 fats in fish oil help us balance out our typically high omega-6 fat intake that is typical in modern, highly processed foods and can actually increase inflammation. Ideally we should have a 4:1 omega-6 to omega-3 fat ratio, but with our reliance on processed seed oils, we usually come far from that ratio. For example, corn oil contains roughly a 45:1 omega-6: omega-3 ratio. It's hard to balance that out through diet alone, and that is where good quality fish oil can come in to help. Of course reducing our omega-6 processed seed oils can be just as, if not more, beneficial in reducing inflammation in the body (i.e., stop eating processed "food").

Recovery Protocols

Even with a solid nutritional program, including strength training with your cycling can add a significant toll on your ability to recover. As we noted previously, it is advisable to combine your strength-training days with your harder-riding days so that you can preserve recovery. You need easy days and off days for your body to recover and continue to improve. It is during periods of recovery that we actually reap the rewards of our workouts. Nutrition is the foundation to the techniques below. Caloric deficits, protein deficiencies, or becoming dehydrated will all drastically impair recovery and ultimately performance.

Dialing in your nutrition and hydration is critical in maximizing your recovery. As an athlete, you shouldn't be going anywhere without a water bottle. Maintaining adequate hydration to restore optimal cell function is the primary concern post exercise. We recommend drinking a total of 16-24 ounces of water for every hour of exercise, including strength training. This is above your normal daily fluid intake. Including some electrolytes, or trace minerals supplement in the fluid will also help absorption.

The techniques below are solid ancillary techniques to maximize recovery, and performance.

> **Ice Bath/Cold Shower.** Who doesn't love a nice cold shower?! Ok, so this doesn't sound like a relaxing experience, but science shows that cold exposure can be extremely beneficial to athletes. Before we dig in on the science behind cold exposure, or cold thermogenesis, it is important to realize that this isn't a new technique. In 2006, when the US Olympic Training Center in Colorado Springs built a dedicated recovery center for the 400+ resident athletes at their facility, they included not only a dry sauna (which is ridiculously hot) but "ice pools" kept at approximately 50 degrees Fahrenheit. Athletes had differing protocols using the two extremes, but all of them included approximately 15 minutes spent in the ice pool. Many athletes would start in the dry sauna to allow blood to move to the skin surface, a normal response to heat exposure to reduce core temperature in a hot environment, then jump into the ice pool to cause rapid cooling of body temperature. The cooling causes the blood to flow deep into muscles and core tissue, bringing nutrients with it as well as eliminating waste products. Both of these processes can drastically help muscle resynthesize.
>
> **Going out in the cold** can actually help immune system function (http://jap. physiology.org/content/87/2/699). Cold can stimulate norepinephrine due to its sympathetic nervous system response, which in turn activates leukocytosis and granulocytosis (natural immune system killer cells) which can improve immune function. That can be especially helpful when doing post-endurance exercise where we typically see an immune system suppression for 1-2 hours prior to longer workouts. (Immune Function in Sport and Exercise, Michael Gleeson, Journal of Applied Physiology Published 1 August 2007 Vol. 103 no. 2, 693-699 DOI: 10.1152/japplphysiol.00008.2007)

While cold exposure is a relatively new branch of study, there does seem to be an up-regulation of hormone receptor affinity for hormone binding (http://www.ncbi.nlm.nih.gov/pubmed/15489860). Essentially, this means your normal hormone release is more effective, resulting in less of the hormone needed for effective change. This may be very helpful in cases where hormone receptors become desensitized from chronic stress, including exercise and emotional/work induced stress.

Moderate cold exposure (15 minute ice baths) can be extremely beneficial in helping athletes recover, handle stress better, and help control body weight. If ice baths are not possible in your schedule, then cold showers can also be used pretty effectively. Ray Cronise (NASA scientist who has done a lot of research on the benefits of cold thermogenesis) has even developed a quick cold shower protocol to make the process a bit faster. Essentially it is five minutes of a warm shower followed by 20 seconds of cold, 10 seconds of warm, repeated 10 times. That is a total of five minutes added to your normal shower time. The frequency of the cold exposure would vary depending on your goals, but if you are using this to help with recovery, I would suggest not using it more than a few times a week. You want the hormesis response (a stressor that results in a positive adaptation) of training to drive adaptation. Techniques that may improve recovery used more frequently may lessen your adaptation to training in the long-term.

Foam Rolling. Using a foam roller is a way to practice self-myofascial release (SMR). Myofascial release is a technique that can reduce pain, restore muscle function, and improve range of motion by applying gentle pressure to the connective tissue and lining of the muscles. This technique can restore mobility through autogenic inhibition. Autogenic inhibition is when the golgi tendon organ, a proprioceptive sensory receptor, senses that tension within the muscle/tendon structure is becoming too high, and to protect the muscle it stimulates the muscle spindles to release, thus lengthening the muscle. Basically this provides the same benefit as passive stretching but also helps improve muscle pliability, and removes soft-tissue adhesions and scar tissue. This restores the sliding surfaces that our layers of muscles and connective tissue require to function optimally. It is possible to get these same results from active release therapy or massage performed by physical therapists, chiropractors, and licensed massage therapists, but these professionals can be pretty expensive to use on a regular basis.

There are a lot of foam rollers out there but the one that I like the best is The Grid from Trigger Point. It is a hard PVC pipe with a textured foam covering. The alternating texture on the roller allows you to adjust the relative firmness of the roller. To have a little more pressure you just roll on the wider grid; to have a little less you roll on the smaller grid. Since the foam roller has the PVC center it won't break down with use, and being only 13" long it travels really well. (I know you will want to take everywhere with you once you start using it!) Basically, this will be the only foam roller you will need to buy.

It should be noted that there are some instances when using a foam roller would be counter-indicated. I would not recommend rolling on areas that have been recently injured, have circulatory problems, chronic pain conditions, or on joints or bony structures.

One other useful tool we recommend picking up is a lacrosse or massage ball. These are roughly the size of a tennis ball but a bit firmer. Being smaller than a foam roller, they can be used to hit areas that the broad surface of a foam roller is too big to address, such as the smaller muscles of the chest, or the lateral hip muscles.

How to Foam Roll: As a general rule, you should spend about 1-2 minutes working on an area. The key is to spend the most time on areas that are tight or slightly more painful. We call these hotspots or trigger points. You can spend less time on areas that don't hurt as much. Use the slight pain as a guide to find what needs the most work. Ideally you should work up to more and more pressure. You can position your body to control the amount of pressure and make subtle changes to get a bit deeper on areas that need it.

IT Band

- Lie on your side with the foam roller underneath the lower lateral portion of your thigh. You can start with the same side elbow and the opposite hand/foot on the ground and progress to stacking both legs to increase pressure.   From the starting position, roll back and forth with controlled movements from the top of the hip to just above the knee.

Quads/Hip Flexor

- Lie on your stomach with the roller underneath the front of one of your thighs and the other leg off to the side. Place your elbows on the ground underneath your shoulders. From the starting position, roll back and forth over the front of your thigh with controlled movements, from the hip to just above the knee. Complete this movement with both the knee straight and bent. After rolling the quad, reposition the roller on the front lateral side of the hip and roll from the top of the femur to the top of the hip bone with slow controlled movements. Repeat on other side.

Leg Adductor (Inside of thigh)

- Lie on your stomach with the roller next to your body. Bend one leg and place your inner thigh on top of the roller.   From this position, roll back and forth over the inside of your thigh from the groin to just above the knee with controlled movements. Repeat on other side.

Gluteus Medius

- Lie on your side with the roller under the back portion of your hip/glutes (butt). Place the same side elbow and the opposite hand/foot on the ground. From the starting position, roll back and forth over the back and outside portion of your hip with controlled movements. Repeat on other side.

Lacrosse Ball Option for Gluteus Medius/Piriformis

- Sit on the ground with a lacrosse ball or massage ball next to one hip on the floor. Cross your right leg over your left and then lift your hips up and on top of the ball so that it is pressing into the side of the right hip/gluteus medius. Slowly move your hips in circles and side to side, working on any trigger points. Repeat on other side. Do not spend more than two minutes on this area per side.

Calves

- Sit on the ground with one leg straight out in front of you with the foam roller underneath your calf. Using your arms, press yourself up so that your butt is hovering above the ground and roll back and forth from the ankle to just below the knee with controlled movements. You can increase the pressure by stacking one leg on top of the other and moving to a lacrosse ball.   Make sure to rotate to hit the inside and outside areas of the calves as well. Repeat on the other side.

Chest

- Stand next to a wall and place massage ball or lacrosse ball on the wall at chest height. Push one side of your chest into the ball to hold it in place and slowly roll back and forth between your shoulder and sternum. Hunt around in this area with the ball as you are likely to find areas that are a bit more tender than others. Repeat on other side.

Lats

* Lie on your side with the foam roller placed in your arm pit. Extend your arm and turn your palm to the ceiling to externally rotate your arm, and slowly roll between your armpit and your lower rib cage with controlled movements. Repeat on other side.

Thoracic Spine or Upper Back

- Lie on your back with a foam roller placed in the middle of your back, right below the scapula (shoulder blades). Your feet and butt should be on the ground with hands placed behind your head. From this position, slowly extend the upper back (towards the ground). Slightly contract your abs to prevent your lower back from moving. With this movement, you aren't rolling on the foam roller. This is simply a pivot point to allow the upper back to extend. Slowly work the roller up and down the back, repeating extension at various spinal levels but never below the shoulder blades.

The Exercises

Lower Body

Front Squat

This exercise is best done in a squat rack for maximum safety. Begin by placing the barbell at shoulder height and begin the movement by bringing your arms under the barbell so it sits on the front of your shoulders. You can either use a cross grip, crossing your arms to hold the bar, or a snatch grip. Straighten your legs and torso to lift the bar off the rack. Using a shoulder width grip with feet straight or slightly turned out, start by pushing your hips back and bending your knees to lower the weight. Make sure you keep your abs and back tight to maintain a neutral spine. Lower the weight as low as you can while maintaining a neutral spine. Do not go past the point where you feel comfortable or start to lose neutral spine, and press the weight back up to the starting position. Make sure you do not let your knees collapse inward when pressing up, or let them come forward farther than the toes.

Front Box Squat Variation

The movement is the exactly the same as above, except place and 18 – 24 inch plyometric box behind you. You will then lower the weight down until you touch the box and press back up to the starting position. Do not bounce off the box.

Goblet Squat

If you are using lower weights or only have dumbbells or kettlebells, than the goblet squat may be a good option. The lower body setup is exactly the same, except instead of using a barbell we will use a dumbbell or kettlebell, holding it like a goblet. Then you squat down, trying to keep elbows over your knees and back up to the starting position.

Deadlift

Many people are worried about getting injured with the deadlift. As with all weight-training exercises, there is risk with this movement, but if you perform the setup that we describe here, it can be relatively safe. It is bad form that causes injuries, not the lift itself. This is also a compound movement, meaning that it uses several joints and muscles. Due to this, you will probably lift the most amount of weight with this movement.

With this movement, we typically see the biggest returns on power development in cyclists. Learning how to properly deadlift and incorporating it into your weight routines is critical for maximizing your time in the gym.

There are books written on how to effectively deadlift. This is just a quick guide, but seek extra guidance if you do not feel comfortable with this movement.

Instruction: To begin, place the barbell on the floor. We typically recommend using Olympic plates for this movement since even at lower weights it keeps the bar at mid-shin length. This prevents having to round the back to reach lower than possible while keeping a flat back.

Begin by placing your feet under the barbell so the barbell is at mid-foot, feet shoulder-width apart, and toes straight or slightly turned out.

Reach down and grab the bar so that your arms are just outside your legs. Bend your knees slowly until your shins hit the bar. Keep your hips high so that there is a gentle stretch in your hamstring. Lift your chest so that your back is straight. Do not let your hips drop. Then begin your pull by pressing your feet into the ground, lifting the bar off the ground, while keeping the bar close to your legs. Do not shrug at the top. Slowly lower the weight down by pushing your hips backward and bend your knees as the bar passes knee height. Keep the bar close to your legs. Do not bounce the weight off the floor between reps.

Deadlift Sumo Variation

The Sumo variation is essentially the same movement with a different setup. With this variation you will begin with your legs spread to about double shoulder width. Your feet should still be straight or slightly toe out. You will grab the bar between your legs and complete the lift as detailed above. This will work slightly different muscles in your hips.

Deadlift Rack-pull Variation

The Rack-pull variation is essentially a half deadlift. The body setup is exactly the same as the standard deadlift but instead of the barbell being on the ground it will be in the lower position of a squat rack at approximately knee height. This allows us to just work on the top portion of the movement, isolating upper back and hip musculature. Most athletes will also be able to lift more weight with this movement versus the deadlift.

One-leg Deadlift Variation

Begin by holding a dumbbell with one hand and standing on the same side leg. Keeping your standing leg knee slightly bento, perform a deadlift motion by flexing at your hip, lowering the dumbbell. Extend your other leg behind you to maintain balance. As a goal, try to lower your torso until parallel to the ground. Then return to a standing position, squeezing your butt on the way back up. Try to limit any twisting while performing this movement. Repeat with other leg.

Bulgarian Split Squat

Using a pair of dumbbells held at your side, stand on one leg with your leg behind you on a bench. You rest the top of your foot on the bench behind you. Brace your core to help stabilization, then squat down by flexing your knee and bring it close to the ground. Your knee should not move forward past your toes. Then press up back to the starting position. Repeat with other leg.

Dumbbell Lunge

Begin by standing upright with two dumbbells held at your sides. Then step forward with one foot, approximately 24 inches in front of you, and lower your body down. Make sure to not let your knee move farther forward than your toes, then press back up through your heel and move your foot back to resume a standing posture. Repeat with other leg.

Barbell Lunge

This is essentially the same movement as the standard Dumbbell Lunge, but with a barbell held as you would for a front squat. This is a bit more challenging to maintain balance and will help with muscle development.

Reverse Lunge

This is essentially the same movement as the standard Dumbbell Lunge, but instead of stepping forward 24 inches, you will step backward 24 inches. This allows for slightly more posterior chain involvement.

Walking Dumbbell Lunge

This is essentially the same movement as the standard Dumbbell Lunge, but instead of moving your foot back to a standing position after doing the lunge, you will bring your foot up so you have taken a step forward.

Hip Bridge

Begin by lying on your back, with your knees bent and feet flat on the floor approximately shoulder width apart. Your hands should be resting at your sides. Pushing through your heels, lift your hips off the floor until your back is straight. Hold this position for one second, then slowly lower your hips back to the floor.

One Leg Hip Bridge Variation

This is essentially the same as the standard Hip Bridge, but you are only using one heel to lift your hips while keeping your other leg straight and parallel to your opposite thigh. Repeat on other side.

Upper Body

Barbell Bench Press

Lie on a flat bench and grab the barbell with a handlebar-width grip. Slowly push up to un-rack the barbell and hold above your body with vertical arms. Then lower the bar towards the middle of your chest by bending your elbows down, not out. Do not bounce the bar off your chest. Briefly pause at the lower position, then press the bar back up to the starting position, holding it extended for one second before repeating for the number of prescribed reps. If you are new to this exercise or pushing a challenging weight, it is advised to use a spotter. If you don't have a spotter, you should use a manageable weight that does not put you at risk.

Alternating Dumbbell Bench Press

This is essentially the same movement as the Barbell Bench Press, but instead of using a barbell, use two dumbbells. Alternate completing one movement with each arm at a time. One rep is considered one press with each arm.

Incline Bench Press

This is essentially the same movement as the Barbell Bench Press, but performed on a bench at an incline so the bench is higher and closer to the bar. We use this to hit slightly different muscles.

Close-grip Bench Press

This is essentially the same movement as the Barbell Bench Press, but done with a grip that is approximately one hand-width apart. This will make the movement much more challenging and use slightly different muscles. Most athletes find they need to reduce the weight 20-30% fom what they use for a typical wider bench press.

Barbell Bent-over Row

Holding a barbell in a standing position with your hands pronated (palms facing toward you). With slightly bent knees, slowly lower your torso until it is as close to parallel to the ground as you can get with a straight back. The barbell should be hanging below you. While keeping your torso stationary, pull the barbell up to your chest while keeping your elbows close to your body. Hold for a brief pause at the top and slowly lower the weight back down.

Dumbbell Bent-over Row: One-arm Variation

This is essentially the same movement as the Barbell Bent-over Row, but done holding two dumbbells and alternating pull them up to your chest. One rep is one row with each arm.

Dumbbell Bent-over Row: One-arm, One-leg Variation

This is essentially the same movement as the standard Dumbbell Bent-over Row, but done standing on one leg. Repeat the number of prescribed reps before switching to the other side.

Pull-up

Grab the pull-up bar with your palms facing away from you and your hands just wider than shoulder-width. From a dead hang, tighten your abs and pull up until your chin is at the bar, then slowly lower back down to a dead hang. If you find it challenging to do a pull-up, you can use a pull-up assist machine, wrap a band around your knee to help lift you up, or just start with an inverted row (next exercise).

Inverted Row

To perform this you will need a lower bar at about waist height. Setting up a barbell in a squat rack or using a Smith machine often works well. Lying underneath the bar, grab the bar with your hands slightly wider than shoulder width, with your palms facing your feet. Your body should be straight with your hips off the ground, and only your heels touching the ground. Then perform a rowing motion. Bring your chest up to the bar and slowly lower yourself back down so your arms are fully extended. Do not let your hips flex or touch the ground throughout the entire set.

118

Push-up

Lie down on your stomach and place your hands slightly wider than shoulder-width, palms straight, and just below your shoulders. Your toes should be under your feet. With your abs and butt tight, push your hands into the ground, keeping your elbows close to your side as your extend your arms. Your head should be looking straight down. Slowly lower yourself, keeping your elbows close to your body. Bring your mid chest down your hands until you gently touch the ground and then press back up.

Clap Push-up

This is essentially the same movement as the standard Push-up, but you will push up explosively so that your hands come off the ground just long enough to clap together. Then they will get back to the starting position in order to slowly lower your chest back down before performing another explosive push. The Clap Push-up is also a plyometric exercise.

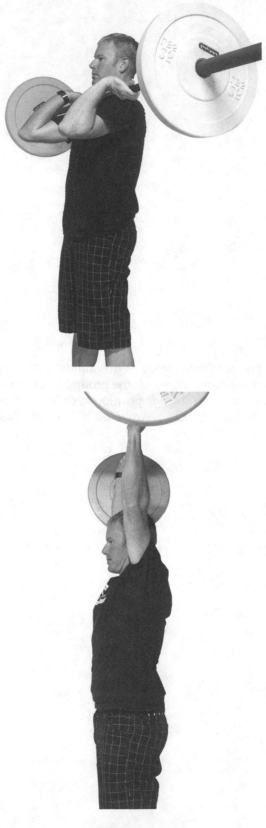

Barbell Push Press

Begin by placing a barbell at chest height in a squat rack. Grab the barbell with your palms facing away from you with a grip slightly wider than shoulder-width. Slightly bend your knees and place the barbell on the front of your shoulders, then lift it off the rack by standing back up. Keep your abs and butt tight, feet shoulder-width apart, and push the barbell up and over your head until your arms are fully extended. Slowly lower the bar back down to your shoulders and repeat for reps.

Dumbbell Push Press

This is essentially the same movement as the Barbell Push Press, but you will use dumbbells held with your palms facing each other. Rest the dumbbells on your deltoids (outside of shoulder) and press upwards until your arms are fully extended. Do not bounce the weight off your shoulders between reps.

Pallof Press

Assume an athletic position with your feet slightly wider than shoulder width, knees slightly bent, shoulders back, and chest tall. Using a cable pull machine with a single hand attachment or a rubber band setup to your side, grab the handle and take a step to your side so that there is tension pulling from your side. Start with your hands close to your chest and press straight out, keeping your shoulders, arms, and hips straight ahead. The cable or band will be trying to rotate your torso, but resist this rotation and maintain a straight alignment. This is the goal of the exercise. Hold for 3-5 seconds and bring your hands back to your chest to complete rep.

Plank

Begin by placing your forearms on the ground directly below your shoulders and push your toes into the ground. Squeezing your butt and abs, assume a plank position with a straight torso. Keep your head straight by looking directly down at the ground and maintain the position with a straight torso for the prescribed duration. You can make this more challenging by extending your arms into a push-up position, or by placing an unstable surface below the arms like a medicine ball.

Side Plank

Lie on your side and place your forearm under your shoulder, perpendicular to your body. Stack your legs on top of each other and extend your hips and knees. Then raise your hips so your body forms a straight line. Maintain position for prescribed time.

Plyometrics

Box Jumps

These are highly advanced and should only be done if you have a very dialed-in squat pattern and are feeling very comfortable with box jumps. You will need one plyometric box that is 20-24 inches tall for this exercise. Begin by standing on the plyometric box with your toes on the edge of the box. Dip down and jump off the box, landing on the ground. As you land on the ground, immediately dip down and explode into the air as high as you can. Try to land with your feet shoulder width apart and with bent knees. Then step back on to the box for the next rep.

Depth Jumps

These are highly advanced and should only be done if you have a very dialed dialed-in squat pattern and are feeling very comfortable with box jumps. You will need one plyometric box that is 20-24 inches tall for this exercise. Begin by standing on the plyometric box with your toes on the edge of the box. Dip down and jump off the box, landing on the ground. As you land on the ground, immediately dip down and explode into the air as high as you can. Try to land with your feet shoulder width apart and with bent knees. Then step back on to the box for the next rep.

Chest-to-Bar Pull Up

This is essentially the same as the standard Pull-up exercise detailed earlier, but done with an explosive pull to bring your chest up to bar height. Do not swing while doing this, and start each pull-up from a dead hang.

Chris Burnham

138

The Workouts and Programs

This is where we put everything together and start to do the physical work. When you start each program is dependent on how you prioritize your cycling season. I would suggest starting with the transition phase, wherever you are in your season, if you are new to weight training or haven't been weight training for a while. As stated earlier, this will help the transition into the gym and limit some of the soreness experienced when starting a strength program.

Transition

Always lift weights before riding. Riding after may help with delayed onset muscle soreness, as will foam rolling in the evening after workouts.

Workout #1

Exercise	Sets	Reps	Tempo	Load	Rest
Box Squats	3	8	Controlled	Bodyweight or <50% RM	60 sec
Deadlifts	3	8	Controlled	<50% RM	60 sec
Walking Lunges	3	8	Controlled	Bodyweight	60 sec
Glute Bridges	3	8	Controlled	Bodyweight	60 sec

Workout #2

Exercise	Sets	Reps	Tempo	Load	Rest
Push-Ups	3	8	Controlled	Bodyweight	60 sec
Pull-Ups	5	3	Controlled	Bodyweight or Band-assisted	60 sec
Inverted Rows	3	8	Controlled	Bodyweight	60 sec
Plank	5	1	Hold for 30 sec each	Bodyweight	30 sec
Pallof Press	3	8	Controlled	50% RM	30 sec

Workout #3

Exercise	Sets	Reps	Tempo	Load	Rest
Deadlifts	4	5	Controlled	60% RM	60 sec
Goblet Squat	3	8	Controlled	<50% RM	60 sec
Bench Press	3	8	Controlled	50% RM	60 sec
Bent Over Rows	3	8	Controlled	50% RM	60 sec
Pull-Ups	5	3	Controlled	Bodyweight or Band-assisted	60 sec

Base Phase 1

This is where we build strength. These are harder workouts and will result in the biggest gains. Always do your weight workouts before riding and make sure that you are taking at least one day off from riding and weights per week to continue making gains. Do not do more than three workouts a week and never on consecutive days.

Workout #1

Exercise	Sets	Reps	Tempo	Load	Rest
Front Squats	4	5	Controlled	70% RM	90 sec
Deadlifts	4	5	Controlled	70% RM	90 sec
Reverse Lunges	3	8	Controlled	60% RM	60 sec
Glute Bridges	3	8	Controlled	Bodyweight	60 sec

Workout #2

Exercise	Sets	Reps	Tempo	Load	Rest
Bench Press	4	6	Controlled	70% RM	90 sec
Pull-Ups	5	3	Controlled	Bodyweight or Band-assisted	60 sec
Inverted Rows	3	8	Controlled	Body Weight	60 sec
Barbell Push Press	3	8	Controlled	60% RM	60 sec
Plank	3	1	1-Min Hold	Bodyweight	30 sec
Side Plank	3	1	1-Min Hold	Bodyweight	30 sec

Workout #3

Exercise	Sets	Reps	Tempo	Load	Rest
Deadlifts	4	5	Controlled	70% RM	120 sec
Front Squat	5	5	Controlled	70% RM	120 sec
Push-Ups	3	8	Controlled	Bodyweight	60 sec
Bent-Over Rows	3	8	Controlled	60% RM	60 sec
Glute Bridge	3	8	Controlled	Bodyweight	30 sec

Base Phase #2

Workout #1

Exercise	Sets	Reps	Tempo	Load	Rest
Sumo Deadlift	5	4	Controlled	80% RM	120 sec
Reverse Lunge	5	5	Controlled	70% RM	90 sec
One-Leg Squat	5	5	Controlled	70% RM	60 sec
Pallof Press	3	8	Controlled	70% RM	30 sec

Workout #2

Exercise	Sets	Reps	Tempo	Load	Rest
Alternating Dumbbell Bench Press	4	6	Controlled	65% RM	60 sec
One-Arm Bent Over Dumbbell Row	5	5	Controlled	65% RM	60 sec
Push-Up	3	8	Controlled	Bodyweight	60 sec
Plank	3	1	1-Min Hold	Bodyweight	30 sec
Side Plank	3	1	1-Min Hold	Bodyweight	30 sec

Workout #3

Exercise	Sets	Reps	Tempo	Load	Rest
Speed Front Box Squat	3	5	Controlled down, explosive up	50% RM	90 sec
Rack Pulls	5	3	Controlled	90% RM	120 sec
Clap Push-Ups	3	5	Explosive	Bodyweight	90 sec
Inverted Row	3	8	Controlled	Bodyweight	60 sec
Pallof Press	3	8	Controlled	80% RM	30 sec

Base Phase #3

Workout #1

Exercise	Sets	Reps	Tempo	Load	Rest
Front Squat	4	5	Controlled	85% RM	120 sec
One-Leg Deadlift	5	5	Controlled	60% RM	90 sec
Walking Lunge	3	8	Controlled	60% RM	60 sec
Pallof Press	3	12	Controlled	70% RM	30 sec

Workout #2

Exercise	Sets	Reps	Tempo	Load	Rest
Bench Press	4	5	Controlled	70% RM	90 sec
Pull-Ups	6	3	Controlled	Bodyweight or Band-assisted	60 sec
Alternating Dumbbell Bench Press	3	8	Controlled	70% RM	60 sec
Plank	3	1	1-Min Hold	Bodyweight	30 sec
Side Plank	3	1	1-Min Hold	Bodyweight	30 sec

Workout #3

Exercise	Sets	Reps	Tempo	Load	Rest
Deadlift	6	3	Controlled	90% RM	120 sec
Bulgarian Split Squat	4	8	Controlled	70% RM	90 sec
One-Arm Bent Over Dumbbell Row	4	5	Controlled	70% RM	90 sec
Dumbbell Push Press	3	8	Controlled	60% RM	90 sec
Clap Push-Up	3	5	Explosive	Bodyweight	90 sec

Explosive Plyometrics

These are very stressful to the central nervous system. These shouldn't be done more than twice per week. Always do plyometrics before riding and never do them when tired.

Workout #1

Exercise	Sets	Reps	Tempo	Load	Rest
Speed Bench Press	4	4	Controlled down, explosive up	60% RM	120 sec
Box Jumps	3	5	Explosive	Bodyweight	120 sec
Glute Bridge	3	8	Controlled	Bodyweight	60 sec
Plank	3	1	1-Min Hold	Bodyweight	30 sec
Side Plank	3	1	1-Min Hold	Bodyweight	30 sec

Workout #2

Exercise	Sets	Reps	Tempo	Load	Rest
Speed Deadlift	3	6	Controlled down, explosive up	50% RM	120 sec
Depth Jumps	2	4	Explosive	Bodyweight	120 sec
Pallof Press	3	15	Controlled	70% RM	30 sec

Workout #3

Exercise	Sets	Reps	Tempo	Load	Rest
Box Jumps	3	5	Explosive	Bodyweight	120 sec
Depth Jumps	2	3	Explosive	Bodyweight	120 sec
Clap Push-ups	2	5	Explosive	Bodyweight	120 sec
Plank	3	1	1-Min Hold	Bodyweight	30 sec
Side Plank	3	1	1-Min Hold	Bodyweight	30 sec

In Season Maintenance

Do not do a weight workout within four days of a race or event. Workout #1 works best on the same day as your hardest riding day. Workout #2 is less stressful and can be incorporated on most riding days. There is no need to do more than two weight workouts per week during the maintenance phase.

Workout #1

Exercise	Sets	Reps	Tempo	Load	Rest
One-Leg Deadlift	4	8	Controlled	50%	60 sec
Split Squat	4	5	Controlled	Bodyweight	60 sec
Alt. Dumbbell Bench Press	3	8	Controlled	60%	60 sec
Pull-Ups	3	6	Controlled	Bodyweight or Band-assisted	60 sec
Plank	3	1	1-Min Hold	Bodyweight	30 sec
Side Plank	3	1	1-Min Hold	Bodyweight	30 sec

Workout #2

Exercise	Sets	Reps	Tempo	Load	
Plank	5	1	45 sec hold	Bodyweight	30 sec
Side Plank	3	1	45 sec hold	Bodyweight	30 sec
Inverted Rows	3	8	Controlled	Bodyweight	30 sec
Pallof Press	3	12	Controlled	50% RM	30 sec
Dumbbell Push Press	3	8	Controlled	50% RM	30 sec

Sample Workout Schedules

Transition

Monday	Tuesday	Wednesday	Thursday	Friday	Saturday	Sunday
Rest Day	Endurance	High Cadence Skill Work	Endurance	Rest Day	Easy Group Ride	Long Endurance
	Transition Weight #1		Transition Weight #2		Transition Weight #3	

Base

Monday	Tuesday	Wednesday	Thursday	Friday	Saturday	Sunday
Rest Day	Threshold Intervals	Endurance	Power Jumps (Low Cadence Jumps)	Rest Day	Group Ride	Long Endurance
	Base Weight #1		Base Weight #2		Base Weight #3	

Pre-Season Plyometrics

Monday	Tuesday	Wednesday	Thursday	Friday	Saturday	Sunday
Rest Day	Endurance	VO2 Max intervals	Endurance	Rest Day	VO2 Max Intervals	Long Endurance
		Plyometrics #1 or #2			Plyometrics #2 or #3	

In Season Maintenance #1

Monday	Tuesday	Wednesday	Thursday	Friday	Saturday	Sunday
Rest Day	Group Ride or Intervals	Endurance	High Cadence Sprint Work	Rest Day	Group Ride	Long Endurance
	Maintenance Workout #1				Maintenance Workout #2	

In Season Maintenance #2

Monday	Tuesday	Wednesday	Thursday	Friday	Saturday	Sunday
Rest Day	Group Ride or Intervals	Endurance	Rest Day	Pre-Race Openers	Race or Event	Endurance
	Maintenance Workout #2					

References

Abt, John P.; Smoliga, James M.; Brick, Matthew J.; Jolly, John T.; Lephart, Scott M.; Fu, Freddie H. (2007), **Relationship between cycling mechanics and core stability.** Journal of Strength & Conditioning Research: November 2007

Bahr R, Sejersted OM. (1991), **Effect of intensity of exercise on excess postexercise O2 consumption. Metabolism.** 1991 Aug; 40(8):836-41.

Bolam KA, van Uffelen JG, Taaffe DR. 2013. **The effect of physical exercise on bone density in middle-aged and older men: a systematic review.** Osteoporos Int. 2013 Nov;24(11):2749-62. doi: 10.1007/s00198-013-2346-1. Epub 2013 Apr 4.

Christie, A., & Kamen, G. (2009). **Gender and age-related training adaptations in maximal motor neuron firing rate.** *ACSM 56th Annual Meeting, Seattle, Washington.* Presentation number 2700.

Cuddy, Amy J.C., Caroline A. Wilmuth, and Dana R. Carney. "**The Benefit of Power Posing Before a High-Stakes Social Evaluation.**" Harvard Business School Working Paper, No. 13-027, September 2012.

Elliot, Diane L., Goldberg, Linn, Kuehl, and Kerry S. "**Effect of Resistance Training on Excess Post-exercise Oxygen Consumption.**" Journal of Strength & Conditioning Research: May 1992

Farinatti, Paulo, Antonio Gil Castinheiras Neto, and Nádia Lima da Silva, "**Influence of Resistance Training Variables on Excess Postexercise Oxygen Consumption: A Systematic Review,**" ISRN Physiology, vol. 2013, Article ID 825026, 10 pages, 2013. doi:10.1155/2013/825026

HENNEMAN, ELWOOD AND CAMILLE B. OLSON2 (1964) **RELATIONS BETWEEN STRUCTURE AND FUNCTION IN THE DESIGN OF SKELETAL MUSCLES** Department of Physiology, Harvard Medical School, Boston, Massachusetts.

Nichols JF, Palmer JE, Levy SS. (2003), **Low bone mineral density in highly trained male master cyclists.** Osteoporos Int. 2003 Aug;14(8):644-9. Epub 2003 Jul 11.

Osterberg KL, Melby CL. **Effect of acute resistance exercise on postexercise oxygen consumption and resting metabolic rate in young women**. Int J Sport Nutr Exerc Metab. 2000 Mar; 10(1):71-81.

Porter C1, Reidy PT, Bhattarai N, Sidossis LS, Rasmussen BB. (2014), **Resistance Exercise Training Alters Mitochondrial Function in Human Skeletal Muscle**. Med Sci Sports Exerc. 2014 Dec 23.

Rønnestad, B. R., Hansen, J., Hollan, I. and Ellefsen, S. (2015), **Strength training improves performance and pedaling characteristics in elite cyclists**. Scandinavian Journal of Medicine & Science in Sports, 25: e89–e98. doi: 10.1111/sms.12257

Warner SE, Shaw JM, Dalsky GP. 2002. **Bone mineral density of competitive male mountain and road cyclists.** *Bone* **30(1):281-6.**

Index